CONCH

CATS

AT ERNEST HEMINGWAY HOME AND MUSEUM

MONA KELLY / LINDA LARSON

Our purpose is to acquaint visitors with the cats who live at the Hemingway House Museum. This book will help you identify the resident cats while you are strolling the grounds and will answer some of your cat questions. We love all animals, even our husbands, but are partial to cats, and have worked at the Hemingway Museum long enough to know one cat from another.

Photography, Design by Mona Kelly, Linda Larson, Werner J. Bertsch
Text by Linda Larson, Mona Kelly.
Copyright 1993 by Mona Kelly, Linda Larson, Werner J. Bertsch
All rights reserved
No part of this book may be reproduced or transmitted in any form or any means, electronic or mechanical, including photocopy, recording, or any information storage and retrieval system, without permission in writing from Conch Cats, and Pro Publishing, Inc..

ISBN 0-9636896-0-6
Published by Conch Cats
405 Olivia St.
Key West, Fl. 33040, USA
Printed in Italy for Pro Publishing, Inc. (305)680-1771

In his book Papa, Hemingway's son Gregory says "Next to us and his wife and his cats, I think my father loved the Pilar (his boat) more than anything on earth."

Hemingway regarded his cats almost as highly as his boat because of their independent attitude and their do as they please lifestyle. He sometimes named his cats for famous people, and many of the fifty cats that reside at the Hemingway House Museum today are named for movie stars, authors, and characters from his writings.

About half the resident cats are Polydactyl, which means they have extra toes. Usually, cats have five front toes and four back toes, but these have six toes and in some rare cases, even seven toes. The extra toes occur mostly on the front paws, where they look like thumbs, but they may appear on the back paws as well, making the back paws look unusually wide. Some people call cats with extra toes double-pawed.

Polydactylism is a dominant gene which affects all breeds of cat. The cats at the Hemingway Museum come in all shapes, sizes, and colors, but do tend to be smaller tha cats in cold climates, because it requires less energy to dissipate body heat from a lesser body surface.

The original polydactyl cats are thought to have been Maine Coon cats, a large breed of cat from the Eastern United States seaboard, which were used on ships to catch mice and rats. They traveled the sea coasts aboard ships, ranging as far North as New Brunswick and Nova Scotia, leaving offspring in their wake.

Dating back even further, it is said that Marie Antoniette's six Angora cats came to America on the ship that she herself missed.

The cats arrived safely and became the progenitors of the Maine Coon cat breed. This large, longhaired, hearty breed of feline were valued on ships because of their excellent hunting abilities, and some were supposedly the original six toed cats. In Europe, polydactyl cats are virtually non-existent, because during Medieval times any cat which was unusual was put to death due to superstitions regarding witchcraft.

Here in the New World, however, six toed cats were considered good luck by sailors. Hemingway was given his first six toed cat by a ship's captain. Some of the cats living at the Museum today are descendants of that original cat. Regardless of their ancestry, the cats that live here at the Hemingway House Museum are indeed lucky. They are fed and cared-for by the museum staff and receive a great deal of love and attention from both staff and visitors to the museum. They are some of the most relaxed, Key West-y, conched-out cats you have ever seen!

Mark Twain and Snowshoes

"We are nicknamed 'The Bookends' because we do everything together. I am the dignified red tabby in the background and am named for one of Hemingway's favorite authors. My friend, Snowshoes, is named for his white paws, which he insists on waving in the breeze while he sleeps. You'd think he had been into the cat-nip! I would know if he had, though, because we're always together."

Trevor Tuxedo

"I am named for my favorite person at the Hemingway Museum and for my formal markings. I am always dressed for dinner and am never late either, as my pear shaped figure will attest. People often accuse me of being pregnant. If I am, it will be in the Guiness Book of Records, because I'm a neutered male cat.

Sitting on my favorite person's lap is pleasant and I can dangle my seven toed paw for all to admire. I also enjoy a walk with my person sometimes. We cats enjoy a short walk in a safe environment and can be very loving, despite our reputations for cool independence. Not only am I affectionate, but very photogenic, as you can see."

Jennifer Jones

Hello, I'm a calico cat. Did you know that almost all calico cats are female, and that the rare male calico is usually sterile?
I am a mother myself, and a good one if I may say so. My cat daughters Rita Hayworth and Gertrude Stein are some of the prettiest, most charming kitties at the Museum. I have also been a foster mother to other kittens and have raised them as my own. My offspring acquire their sweet, affectionate nature from me. I'm not above standing on my back legs to encourage people to stroke me. You have to look to find me, though, because I spend most of my time near the garage to the rear of the property. Maybe you will meet me and my family someday".

John Dos Passos

"I'm named for Hemingway's Paris friend and fellow author. He is the person who told Hemingway about Key West in the late 1920's.
I am a part vegetarian cat who loves tomato wedges, particularly if they are dipped in tuna salad. I like broccoli and cauliflower, cooked, and even lettuce depending on the type of dressing on it. We cats have diversified tastes you know. I have known cats who liked yogurt, sweets, and even cantaloupe. My opinion is that if we want to try something different, people should let us. They say my sparkling clean fur and purr-fect health are the result of my vegetarian preferences."

Marilyn Monroe

Beautiful, aren't I? My big blue eyes, unique coloring, and smarmy personality make me totally photogenic. Siamese and tabby is what I am. My hobby is sneaking into the house, and I'm an expert. I wait for the hostess to open the door and say 'come in' to the visitors, and then I zoom into the Museum like she's talking to me! Often I go on the tour, I could give the tour, but who wants to work? I prefer to spend my days doing what I want. Notice how cleverly I have hidden myself with the rest of the cats here in the gift shop. Do you think they see me?"

Marlene Dietrich

"I was named for Hemingway's friend, the beautiful actress and singer. They met while both were on a cruise ship and she would not join a dinner party because her presence would have made the number in the party thirteen and she was superstitious. Hemingway gallantly offered to join the party too, thus making the number present fourteen. A lifelong friendship was formed and she always called him Papa.

My lifelong friend is my sister Colette, the cat. We look quite different though, she has long hair and regular toes, while I have short hair and extra toes. We have in common our tabby coloring and our big green eyes."

Colette

"My namesake was a French author and she liked cats too. People say I look like two cats sewn together, or like a Maine Coon cat crossed with a raccoon. What's wrong with them, don't they know that is genetically impossible? I don't know where I got my coloring but I am sort of tabby and ruddy mixed into one. My hobbies include eating, which I do a lot of, napping, and singing. I don't really sing, but if you itch me near the base of my tail, I will lip sync while swinging my head from side to side. Keep that to yourself though, or they may put me to work at the famous Key West sunset celebration."

thello

"Even though I'm a girl cat, I was named Othello. I am jet
black like the Shakespearean character. Perhaps Hemingway
admired Shakespeare's work, I'm sure he read it since he loved
to read.

How I ended up with a boy's name is a good question. Guess
it is difficult to judge young kittens, even though the cat books
say you can tell by the amount of space between those holes
back there. Girl cats have less space between the holes,
according to them. Anyhow, Othello is my name and I do
answer to it, if I feel like it. I take very good care of myself, as
my pear shaped figure and shiny black fur will attest. Somebody
has to do it. I like to sit on a chair on the front porch and bat
my big green eyes. Some person will come by and pet me, you
can bet on it. On cold days, I'll find a warm lap, whether or not
the owner appreciates cats, after all, these are my chairs I'm letting them use. I live here! My only problem is that sometimes my tail
itches and I am too fat to make a U-turn to get to the exact spot. I find that if I drag my tail along someone's shins, they usually get the
hint and give me a good itch. This is extremely helpful, but I am careful not to act pathetically grateful, like some dog might. One has to
maintain a sense of decorum you know. My attitude has gotten me where I am today, and seven toes on my front feet doesn't hurt
either."

Rita Hayworth

"I'm named for a lovely actress who starred in some of the movies
adapted from Hemingway's works. I like to think I'm as pretty as my
namesake with my long, gray, pink tinged fur and my big amber eyes.
I bat those eyes fetchingly if I want people to pay attention to me--it
works. I am particulary fond of any type of treat and can be found
almost anywhere on the Museum grounds vigilantly on the look-out
for hand-outs. I am noted for my cleverness at exposing one claw and
extending my polydactyl paw under another cats nose, then I snag the
treat and it's in my mouth before that other cat knows what
happened. This little touch of greed is my only character flaw,
otherwise I'm considered very sweet tempered."

Katherine Hepburn A.K.A. Sunshine

I'm a little, yellow, tabby cat and consider myself as pretty and elegant as my
namesake. Don't ask me where this confusion regarding my name commenced-
-I don't know, I don't answer to either name anyway. I do like to think that I
bring sunshine into people's lives by sharing my bench with them. My territory
is around the bench near the front gate and if someone rests on my bench, I
inch closer and closer to them until pretty soon I'm right on their lap!

Mr. Bett[

"I was originally named Betty Davis because I have pretty eyes. I was very shy as a kitten due to a traumatic experience I had whe[
I became trapped in the eaves of Mr. Hemingway's writing studio. It's a good place to contemplate writing skills, no doubt, but[
was cat-atonic with fear after all the pounding, prying, and human contact needed to achieve my release. They said I would die[
they left me in the eaves, but if you ask me, they were trying to kill me! I headed for the bushes with haste when they freed me.[
have since made a few friends both four legged and two legged and have decided that humans are not all bad. Quite some tim[
later the staff at the Museum caught me doing something very unladylike and they realized they had a mistake in judging m[
gender. Thus, I became Mr. Betty[

Liz Taylor

"It is said that I resemble a Maine Coon cat, only I'm smaller. People say I'm fat, but
I prefer to think 'I'm too short for my weight.' My most embarrassing incident
occurred when I was cat-napping on the tin roof of the pool patio and decided to
go down for a drink of water. Misjudging the pitch of the roof--guess I was not yet
awake--I began to slide tovard the edge overhanging the pool. I had a drink of water
in mind, not a bath in the stuff, so I put my claws out! The scre-e-ch of my claws on
that tin roof got the attention of everyone nearby, so of course, they were witness
to my cat-apult right into the swimming pool! I made 'quite a splash', if I say so
myself. I swam like a Tiger to the edge, my six toes on all four feet acting as
paddles. I dragged myself out, and proceeded to take a bath like nothing even
happened. One has to do what they can to save dignity in the face of all that
humiliating laughter. But once a star, always a star, I say."

8

Hadley Richardson

"I'm named for Hemingway's first wife....he had four of them you know. People notice me because of my light blue eyes and Siamese coloring, although I have blotches on my coat. I have polydactyl paws and like to cat-nap in the side yard where it's quiet. If I want recognition, I just march to the feeding station on the back porch, where there is petting and food to be had. It always works."

Willard Scott

"Hi-I'm named for that nice weather man on T.V. who acknowledges long-lived persons on their birthdays. I'm not old enough to be on T.V. with the real Willard, but hope to be if I don't have too many experiences like the one I'm about to relate.

One day I was wandering by the pool and stopped to be admired by three visitors. I received the shock of my life when one of them picked me up and tossed me into the water. One of the others had their camera ready to photograph my terror stricken puss as I swam rapidly to the ledge and scrambled to safety. I ran, dripping wet across the whole acre of grounds to escape those people. As I fled, I heard one of the tour guides telling them 'that the cats are not here to be abused'. It's nice to have friends, even if they are a bit late sometimes. Luckily, most of our visitors are much kinder, or it could take years off my life."

Chicken

This is not a cat! It is one of the resident chickens that live in Old Town Key West. Some of these fowl do not know the difference between day and night and will crow at all hours, annoying visitors and locals alike. Since the whole island has been designated a bird sanctuary, even chickens are protected by law. The cats are not aware of this fact and will attempt to prey on them. The baby chicks can be captured by an enterprising feline hunter, but the adult chickens are very intimidating with their loud squawking and wing flapping.

Mo Kitty

"People say I look like an Ocicat, a new breed of cat which looks like a wild African cat, because of my stripes and spots. I am very relaxed and can sleep anywhere at any time. Visitors frequently have to step over me on the walkways. Occasionally, I get hungry for a little chicken dinner, so I slink across the street to where the chickens live. One day lately, I had my eye on some of these biddies, as the little appetizers are called in our neighborhood when the mother hen became aware of my presence. The next thing I knew, I was wearing a Hen Hat! It made me so nervous, I had to go take a nap."

U.S.#
"I'm named for the highway which begins way up North in the state of Maine and ends right here on Whitehead Street in K West, not far from the Hemingway Museum. I am a short haired white cat with black spots thrown on me

Spencer Tracy

"He was the actor who played Santiago, the fisherman, in the movie The Old Man and the Sea. Hemingway wrote that book, and won the Nobel Prize for his contribution to literature in 1954, due in part to that novel.

I am a longhaired tabby cat and I keep to myself and mind my own business. Cat-napping is what I do best, and here I am, showing you how it's done. Anywhere, anytime is my motto."

mokey Robinson

"I'm named for a popular singer, but my voice is nothing like his. My fur is long nd smoke colored, though, hence the name. I have large yellow eyes and a tiring personality."

Sylvia Kitty

"My name was Sylvester for quite a while. During that time, I kept to myself and observed the activities at the Hemingway Museum. Then, one day I had kittens and was renamed Sylvia. Motherhood proved a full time job for me, but eventually the four legged fur balls grew up and left me alone. Suddenly, the humans began to pay a great deal of attention to me. It must have been because I lost my "babyfat" so to speak, and had regained my girlish figure. I was not interested in contact, however, because I was not sure where those kittens came from, and I was not about to take any unnecessary chances. My downfall was my weakness for liverwurst. Before I knew it, my caretakers had captured me and I was on the way to the animal hospital. When I woke up, I was home again and haven't had any kittens since. This experience did not dampen my enthusiasm for liverwurst however, and I discovered that if I hang around the rest of the staff they sometimes share their treats with me. The attention isn't bad either. Isn't life grand?"

13

Gertrude Stein

"is my name. I am named for Hemingway's friend and mentor from his Paris days. She helped him get his start as a writer by reading and critiquing his work and introducing him to other famous artists of that time.

But getting back to me, I'm a calico cat and am sort of an unusual color. My fur is white with pink and gray spots. I have polydactyl paws, but my distinguishing feature is my little half mustache".

Hemingstein

" I am named for one of Hemingway's nicknames and also for my mother Gertrude Stein, the cat. Hemingway enjoyed playing with words and often gave friends and family aliases.

I'm a distinguished looking fellow with a purr-fect mustache inherited from my mother. She is responsible for my extra toes as well. Those toes got me into some trouble recently, when one of the humans tried to take my footprints. She did! Why would I lie? I was treated like a common cat burglar. That woman put my paw in some paint and put me down on some paper. I galloped off with paint a-fly. Got that paint all over her too, I'm happy to say. Then she grabbed me and took me to that pit where water runs and turned on the faucet. The nasty, wet stuff poured out and I struggled valiantly to escape. I was sure she planned to add insult to injury by getting me wet. But she only washed the paint off my paw and set me free. I was so relieved to have eluded a total wetting, that I have almost forgiven her-but not quite."

Ida Lupina

"She was a film star back before my time, but that's who I'm named for. Sometimes I leave my tail lying around. I'm as forgetful as the next one, but when someone inadvertently steps on it, I yowl like a wounded Banshee--it hurts! This occurrence is a serious cat-astrophe, but I try to keep my conch-cat cool and not send anyone limping off on a bloody stump. I am a bit retiring, but sometimes join the tour groups and escort them through the backyard."

Ginger Rogers

"I am pretty cute, just ask me. I may have to lie in the middle of the walkway to get people to notice me, but the threat of being stepped on is worth the extra petting. Take note of the way I use to display my polydactyl paws. This technique was acquired when I was a kitten, because the tour guides were always pulling my paws from under my prone body during nap-time to exhibit my toes. I learned to just nap in this position so they need not bother me while I'm busy.

My pet peeve is being picked-up from the ground--I hate it! When I was a kitten, I would make all my legs rigid whenever someone lifted me off the ground. I was dubbed "Super Kitty",

and everyone within hearing would laugh. Being laughed at is worse than having my nap disturbed, it is intolerable as far as we cats are concerned. I stared at those laughers and gave them rapid blinks which signify extreme displeasure. This body language is as close as a cat can get to a dirty look. The "Super Kitty" part was O.K., we all like a little flattery, but being laughed at is out of the question. So do not try to pick me up."

Denise

"I don't know whether I'm a calico cat or a tortoiseshell cat, a bit of each I guess. I also don't know whether I like to be petted or not, so I squeak when people touch me. The pool patio is my space, but some people don't know about that and are always getting on my chair when I get off it for a moment to get a snack. Humans often comment that I'm built like a fireplug, but I ignore them. I know that they are just trying to offend me so that I will pout off somewhere, leaving my chair in the shade in close proximity to the food bowl. I'm too smart for that, I know what it is to have it 'made in the shade'."

Billy Holiday

"I am a tiny black, longhaired cat, but don't let my size fool you. I am as tenacious as a pro-football player when it comes to racing to get to any type of goody being handed out. I can zoom in like lightening and snatch any appealing tidbit before the other cats know what happened. People find it truly amazing that such a little thing like myself can be so successful at beating out other felines twice my size. Guess I am just as determined as my namesake, the famous Blues singer."

J.R.

"I'm a dignified black and white fellow, who can be found almost anywhere in the neighborhood. I like to visit, but know where home is when it comes to meals. I also know how to make myself scarce when there is flea spraying, ear mite medicine, or worm pills being handed out. It takes a very special treat to entice me to be present during those nasty episodes. Fortunately, I am the picture of health, despite my aversion to human attention--guess I'm just a lucky guy."

Sarah Bernhardt

"was a French actress and author who enjoyed a long illustrious career in Paris, where Hemingway spent several years and began his writing profession.
I am a short haired black cat with white markings. People often say I resemble Sox, the new feline resident at the White House."

Zsa Zsa

"I am a sweet tempered Siamese looking cat, and like many of my co-residents at the Hemingway Museum, I love attention. I will find warm lap anytime and proceed to soak up any affection offered. I get a lot of it too, because I'm a pretty kitty."

harlie Chan

'Pssst--I'm trying to keep a low profile, like my namesake the famous detective. The reason is a cat-egorical error I committed. You ow how we cats will sometimes spray objects as a means of marking territory and also as a means of communicating with others of r species. Well, a lady visitor at the Museum laid her sweater down on the ground while she took a picture. I came along and noticed e strange object and gave it a squirt, to make it blend better with the surroundings. She let out a big yelp, which scared me away, we ts hate loud noises. Guess she didn't want to wear that particular scent of perfume. Somebody put vinegar on it to expel the smell. n in hiding until they forget my indiscretion."

Pumpk

"They named me because of my marmalade coloring and I'll adm
I was somewhat round as a kitten. I have a high self estee
regardless of my name, and consider myself 'The King' on th
Museum grounds. I am a pretty busy guy around here since I'm on
of the few of us who still has all my assets, if you get my drift. M
job is to patrol the area, spray my signature, and discoura
intruders from trying to join the "good life" we residents enjoy
don't like these stray fellows trying to date my girlfriends, wh
knows where they got their genes? Paranoia occasionally sets
when the humans pay too much attention to me. I'm aware th
they may attempt to have me neutered eventually, because all th
catting around is dangerous health-wise, but it will sure spoil n
fur

Asa Tift

"I'm named for the wealthy shipbuilder who constructed this
home back around 1850. I'll bet he was a handsome fellow too
like me. I look Siamese, but could not be a purebred since I am
an outdoor cat. I am not neutered because of my extra toes an
I spend a great deal of my time patrolling my
territory, expounding my virtues by way of scent and announci
myself with loud "merouws" to let the girls know I'm available.
pays to advertise, you know. It also pays to avoid those human
because I've noticed that some of the fellows around here are
missing some parts, if you know what I mean, and my sixth
sense tells me those humans have something to do with it. We
enough said, I need to be on my way, it took Mr. Tift three yea
to get this house built and I don't want it to take me that long t
get a date!"

Pandora

"I am a poolside cat, usually found asleep in one of the flowerpots.
Tell me I don't know how to live! If there is one thing we cats value,
it is a comfortable mattress, much to the ongoing dismay of the
gardeners. They will get a nice, bushy plant going and before they
know it, somebody has made a bed of it. Why are they called
flowerbeds, if a cat is not allowed to use them? I have awakened
from my nap to exhibit one of the ways to use the cat fountain. I
like my water nice and fresh."

Primitive Cat-Picasso Cat-French Lalique Cats

Not all the cats are alive at the Hemingway House Museum, but are beautiful and elegant nonetheless.

Joe Russell

was Hemingway's friend, fishing buddy, and the owner of Sloppy Joe's Bar where the famous author sometimes visited to relax and collect writing material. He is the person they named me for.

People often ask if there are any rats or mice around the Museum. I'm here to tell you that I personally saw one. It was a novel experience for me. Apparently there are tree rats which live up in the palm trees. I don't pay them much mind, since I'm as well fed as the next cat here. One day the repairman came to fix the soda machine, and discovered a 'rat in the works.' The rat escaped to the corner by the guest house with some of us in pursuit. That tree rat reared up on it's hind legs and actually

bared its teeth and growled. Several of us were so startled by this show of bravado, we jumped back momentarily, giving the beast a chance to make its escape. It was a shameful display of cowardice and lack of hunting prowess, so we began to bathe, trying to act as if nothing had happened, but mainly to clean between our toes where a cat's sweat glands are located. I'd sure like another encounter with that smart-alecky rat!"

19

Edgar Allen Poe

"Is my name and I am the largest black cat at the Museum. The famous author I'm named for liked to write some scary stories, but don't be afraid of me, I'm very friendly. I have a cat-osincracy too, we could have called it an idiosyncracy, but we cats are very particular about what we are called. We prefer more flattering titles having to do with our charm and good looks.

Notice how I put my paw in the water bowl and lick water off my paw. Putting my 'paw in it', so to speak, gives me a sense of depth perception. I am the only cat with this method who lives here. You can call me unique, that is a flattering word. The lovely blue and white bowl I'm drinking from is a replica of those used by the Hemingway's to feed and water their cats when they lived in Key West."

Bubba

"My name is a Southern nickname which means friend, or close as a brother. I am very friendly, so the name fits. As you can see, I'm also a typical conched-out, Key West-y cat. I'm a tabby cat with white feet."

Boise

"Hemingway's third home was in Ketchum, Idaho an[d] am named for the capital of that state. He enjoyed Idah[o] because he liked to hunt and fish there. It was at his ho[me] in the West that he died in 1961 when he was sixty on[e] years old.

My fur is an unusual color called Smoke, because the undercoat is white and the tips of my fur are black. I ha[ve] markings and extra toes and can be found lounging in [the] side yard near the area filled with ground cover."

Shadow

"is my name and being elusive is my game. Guess they named me this because I act like I'm afraid of my own shadow. Well, I am all black and am thinner than most of those fatties who live at the Museum. I get more exercise than they do, because I'm on the move a lot, checking to see what's happening in the area. I would like to think of myself as more of a news-cat than a scaredy-cat. Occasionally I do approach people to get a little 'attention fix' but I am basically a loner."